Contents

Hair

How hair grows

Hair is made up of a **protein** called keratin. It is extremely strong – a single strand of hair can be stretched to another one-fifth of its length before it will break. In the diagram below, you can see the different layers that make up each single strand of hair.

We have, on average, between 100,000 and 150,000 hairs on our head. Each day about 50 to 100 hairs fall out making way for new hair to grow. Hair grows approximately 1 cm every month. There are many myths about hair growth, most of which are not true. Brushing your hair 100 times a day, for example, will not make it grow any faster.

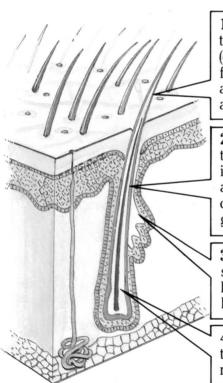

1 Hair is made up of three layers. The cuticle (outer layer) is responsible for protecting the hair against everyday dust and grime.

2 The second layer is the cortex. This gives hair its shine and texture. It also contains a substance called melanin which gives hair its colour.

3 Oil from the sebaceous glands makes hair supple and can affect how greasy it is.

4 The central layer is the medulla and is mostly spongy tissue.

A diagram illustrating the three layers that make up each strand of hair.

Hair growth begins deep down in the scalp where the cells multiply and harden into hair strands. The strands appear through tiny **follicles**, the shape of which affects whether each hair will be curly or straight. Follicles have **sebaceous glands** attached to them. Oil, known as sebum, from the sebaceous glands makes hair healthy and shiny and affects how greasy or dry it is.

HAIR AND MAKE-UP

Christine Green

Wayland

Costumes and Clothes

Accessories
Children's Clothes
Clothes in Cold Weather
Clothes in Hot Weather
Fashionable Clothes
Hair and Make-up
How Clothes Are Made
Sports Clothes
Theatrical Costume
Traditional Costume
Uniforms
Working Clothes

Some words in this book are
printed in bold. Their meanings
are explained in the glossary on
page 30.

Editor: Deborah Elliott
Designer: Ross George
Cover: Pop singers Pepsi and Shirley have their hair designed in modern and
fashionable styles.

First published in 1989 by Wayland (Publishers) Ltd
61 Western Road, Hove, East Sussex BN3 1JD

© Copyright 1989 Wayland (Publishers) Ltd.

British Library Cataloguing in Publications Data
Green, Christine
    Hair and Make-up,
    1. Man. Skin. – For children
    2. Man. Hair. – For children
    I. Title   II. Series
    612'.79

    ISBN 1–85210–380–9

Phototypeset by Kalligraphics Ltd, Horley, Surrey
Printed in Italy by G. Canale C.S.p.A., Turin
Bound in France by A.G.M.

Right The natural colour of hair can be changed by using chemicals to strip the melanin (the substance which gives hair its colour) from the hair and then using more chemicals to produce a new colour.

Below Every one of us has different coloured and textured hair. Look at the various hair types and colours in this photograph.

Hair types

No two people have exactly the same hair – it differs in colour and **texture**. However, everyone has either dry, greasy or normal hair. It is important to know which category your hair falls into when choosing a shampoo or **conditioner**.

Dry hair

Dry hair often looks rather dull and brittle and is usually difficult to manage. If you have dry hair try not to wash it too often. In order to increase the amount of sebum in your hair, brush it regularly and use a conditioning treatment such as olive oil massaged into your scalp.

Greasy hair

Many young people have greasy hair. This is because their sebaceous glands are producing too much sebum. Washing your hair regularly with a mild shampoo will help to reduce the grease.

Normal hair

People who have normal hair should wash and condition it regularly using the correct shampoo and conditioner. Normal hair is shiny and smooth because the right amount of sebum is spread through it.

Bleaching hair too often damages the outer layer, or cuticle, and makes it very dry and brittle.

Normal hair is shiny, smooth and very glossy. To keep it in this condition, wash your hair regularly with a mild shampoo or a shampoo that is specially for normal hair. Use only a small amount of shampoo. Dilute it in half a glass of warm water, apply it thoroughly to all the hair, rinse and allow your hair to dry naturally if possible.

Many people suffer from one of the following hair problems: dandruff, split ends and head lice. All these conditions can be treated.

Dandruff

People who suffer from dandruff can feel very **self-conscious**, because the flakes of dry skin are often noticeable. Dandruff is a build-up of dead skin cells on the scalp. The most effective way to treat dandruff is to wash your hair often using a mild shampoo. There are a number of anti-dandruff shampoos available, but be very careful when selecting one, and be sure to read the list of things that the shampoo contains. If it contains a strong **antiseptic** then avoid buying it, because this ingredient may irritate or even damage the scalp.

Split ends

These can be caused by using a hair dryer that is too hot or by brushing your hair too roughly. The only way to get rid of split ends is to have your hair trimmed regularly – every two or three months.

Lice

Head lice are always thought of as being dirty, and as something only people who do not clean their hair probably suffer from. In fact, nothing could be further from the truth – lice are attracted to clean hair.

Lice are tiny insects which lay eggs on the scalp. They are very difficult to get rid of and are extremely **contagious**. There are many lotions available that will kill the eggs. You have to leave the lotion on your hair for a while and then comb the dead eggs out.

Caring for hair

Before washing your hair gently comb it through to remove any dirt, grease and dead cells. Wet your hair with warm water and then pour a small amount of shampoo into the palm of your hand. Using your fingertips massage the shampoo into your scalp with circular movements. Rinse your hair with plenty of warm running water until there is no trace of soap left. To dry your hair, pat it gently with a towel. Do not rub your head.

Conditioning hair

To keep hair healthy and in good condition use a conditioner after each wash. You can buy a conditioner which is specially suited to your hair type in any chemist's shop.

Conditioning your hair also helps when combing out any tangles. Apply conditioner to your hair and not to your scalp.

Above **Apply conditioner to the ends of your hair, and comb it through without touching the scalp.**

Right **When blow drying hair, hold the dryer about 15cm from your head.**

Drying hair

The best way to dry your hair is to leave it to dry naturally. If you wish to use a hand-held dryer remember to hold it about 15 cm (6 ins) from your head, otherwise it will damage your hair. Before drying your hair use a comb to divide it into sections, then pin each section out of the way. Beginning at the neck, lift up a section of hair at a time using a round brush. Keep the brush close to the scalp and direct the hair dryer at the brush, moving it down from the root to the end. Dry the rest in this way, a section at a time.

What makes a good hairdresser?

It is extremely important to find a good hairdresser. He or she will first study your hair texture before it is washed and check its overall condition. He or she will also offer advice and hopefully give you a haircut which you will be able to cope with easily at home.

Try to remember, however, that hairdressers cannot change your hair type, they can only make the best of what you already have. Many people like to take photographs of the particular hairstyle they want along to their hairdresser. It may be possible, depending on your hair type, to give you that hairstyle. However, hairdresser's cannot actually make you look exactly like the person in the photograph.

Look out for signs in hairdressing salon windows which advertize for models to come and have their hair cut by junior stylists. Most salons need human models for their juniors to practice on. This can be a good way to get a cheap haircut. However, before the junior begins to cut your hair, make sure they are being watched by a trained stylist.

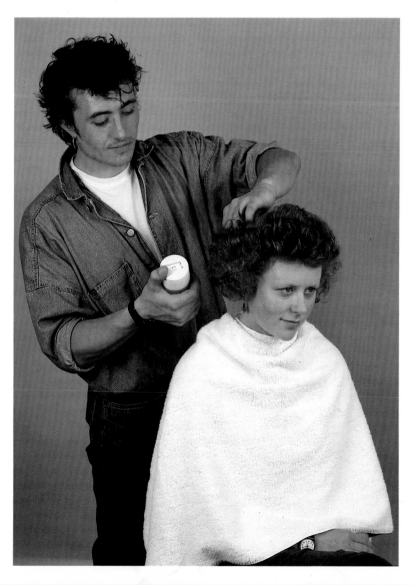

Before going to a hairdresser ask yourself a number of questions. What sort of hairstyle do you want? Is that hairstyle right for you? Are you able to spend a lot of time each morning styling your hair? Spend a few minutes, before the hairdresser begins, talking to him or her about what kind of hairstyle would be best for you.

Finding a style

Before choosing a hairstyle or going to the hairdressers to have your hair cut, take a good look at your hair and decide what type it is. Is it thick and heavy, fine or medium? Is it curly, straight or does it have a slight wave? Then look at your face and decide what shape it is – for example, is it round, long, square, thin or heart-shaped? When you have decided on your hair type and face shape it should be easier to find a style that will suit you.

Right **The 'flat top' hairstyle, fashionable in the 1940s and 1950s, is popular again today.**

Below **A fashionable, spiky hairstyle (left) and an example of a classical 'short back and sides' cut.**

Right When choosing a hairstyle, think about the clothes you wear, your personality and the image you wish to put forward. 'Punk' hairstyles (left) can look dramatic and interesting. However, the style requires enormous amounts of backcombing, gel and hairspray, and these can all damage hair.

Simple, straight hairstyles emphasize the shape of the face. Wash-in colourants, which do not actually dye the hair but tint the colour, can make the styles more interesting.

If you have naturally curly hair, choose a style that is simple and not too fussy to make the most of the curl.

Good and bad habits

In order to have good, healthy hair it is helpful to remember the following:

ALWAYS:
- use your own brushes and combs. Make sure you wash them at least once every week.
- brush out any gel, hairspray or mousse each night.
- cover hair (especially if it is permed or dyed) with a scarf in very hot weather to prevent it from drying out.
- use the correct shampoo for your hair type and follow it up with the correct conditioner.

NEVER:
- comb tangled hair directly from the roots. Start a little way down easing the tangles free as you go.
- pull hair tightly back and hold it in place with rubber bands. Use covered elastic bands.
- keep the hair dryer in one position for too long as it will damage the roots of your hair.
- be tempted to cut your own hair.

When tying your hair up, use elastic bands covered with a soft material. It is best not to use rubber bands because these split and tear the hair.

Always remember to cover your hair with a scarf or a hat in hot sunshine to prevent it from drying out or becoming brittle.

To keep your hair healthy and in good condition follow a balanced diet containing plenty of vitamins and minerals; take plenty of exercise and try to get lots of fresh air.

OTHER USEFUL ADVICE:
- follow a healthy, **balanced diet**.
- do not use too many **electrical appliances** on your hair. Leave it to dry naturally now and again.
- give your hair a good conditioning treatment by putting olive oil on it and leaving it overnight. Wash it out with shampoo the next day.
- exercise frequently.

Colour and perming

It is always advisable to go to a trained hairdresser if you wish to colour, bleach or perm your hair as the chemicals used in these processes can not only weaken your hair but can often actually damage it.

Permanent colour

Dyeing hair is achieved by using a **colourant**. The solution enters the hair shaft and changes the natural colour of the hair. Permanent hair dyes will not wash out but as new hair grows the natural colour will appear again at the roots.

Semi-permanent colour

This type of hair colouring is actually shampooed into the hair and remains for about six washes before beginning to fade. Unlike permanent hair dyes, semi-permanent colours do not enter the hair shaft but simply stick to the outer layer colouring the natural shade.

Bleaching

This process actually involves stripping the hair of its own colour to make it blonde, almost white. Although bleached hair can look quite effective, the chemicals used in the process can seriously damage

Hair that has been bleached blond or white can look effective. However, after only a few weeks dark roots begin to appear. If the roots are bleached too often, the hair becomes dry and brittle.

Left The main advantages of having permed hair are that your hair will gain body, curl and style and will be a lot easier to manage. The disadvantages, however, are that perming can seriously damage your hair if it is not done properly. It can also prove disastrous if you do not like the perm because it will take up to three months to grow out.

Below Colouring your hair can achieve many different effects. You could have a subtle tint, or you could be really adventurous and have permanent multi-coloured streaks.

both skin and hair. Also, dark roots soon begin to show through on dramatically bleached hair, so you will have to keep dyeing it regularly.

Perming

Perms (permanent waves) are special treatments in which part of the hair structure is broken down. The hair is then reset in a different shape using rollers. Remember that perms can last up to three months, so if you do not like the result you will have to put up with it for quite a while.

Henna

This is a natural colourant which will give your hair an overall reddish tint. The good thing about henna is that it will not damage your hair.

Equipment to use

A great many hair problems are
caused by using the wrong equipment.

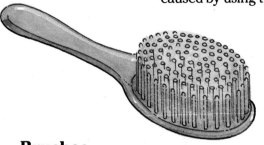

Brushes

A well cared for brush, washed
frequently and the hairs removed with
an old toothbrush, should last for
about five years. There are many on
the market but those with rounded
quills are far kinder to the scalp.

Combs

The ideal comb has wide-spaced teeth
and flat edges which will not harm the
hair.

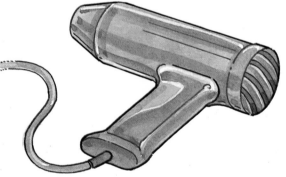

Heated rollers

Heated rollers are portable, quick, and
give excellent results. Although, if they
are used too much they can dry out the
hair. They are best used on damp hair
and left to cool before removing.

Hair dryer

When buying a new hair dryer choose
one which: has two speeds; is light and
easy to handle; has a removable
nozzle to offer more distribution of
heat.

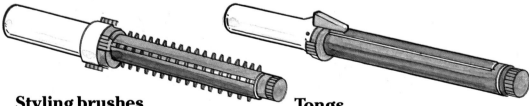

Styling brushes

Unlike tongs styling brushes are used
to give bounce. For best results use on
damp hair.

Tongs

These are very useful in finishing off a
hairstyle. They can make straight hair
curly.

Above To keep hair in good condition it is important to use the proper equipment. Also, always be sure to clean your brush or comb regularly and thoroughly because dirt and grease can collect in the teeth.

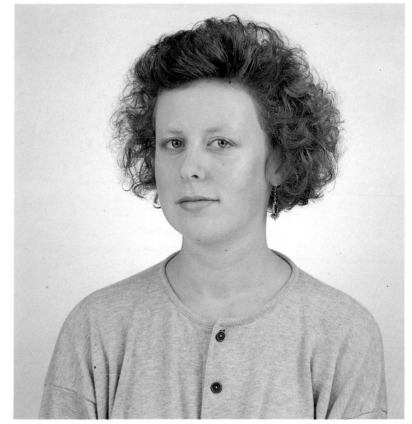

Right To give a medium-length 'bob' a tousled effect, blow dry the hair away from the face, and use a styling brush to give bounce and curl.

Skin

How skin is made

Skin is very important: it protects our muscles from damage and **infections**; it is waterproof; and it lets us feel things such as heat and cold.

Skin is made up of several layers. The most important are the dermis (the inner area) and the epidermis (the outer area).

Epidermis

The outer epidermis is the top layer of skin where the sebaceous glands are located. New skin cells are constantly being formed in the epidermis as dead cells are worn away. It also acts as a protector and prevents germs from getting inside.

Above **Skin is very important because it acts as a barrier against infections. Good, healthy-looking skin can also be a very important asset. So, whether you were born with a perfect complexion, or one that is not so good, you should take care of it properly.**

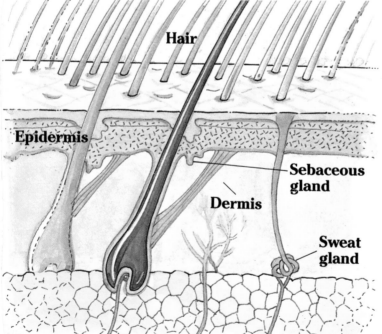

Hair

Epidermis

Sebaceous gland

Dermis

Sweat gland

This illustration shows the different layers that make up our skin.

During adolescence the body undergoes a number of changes and this can often have a bad effect on skin. If you have spots you should not squeeze them, otherwise you will spread the infection and cause more spots to appear. Blackheads can be squeezed, but only after a hot bath when all the pores are open. Remember to apply antiseptic cream afterwards to keep the skin clear.

Dermis

The dermis is the thick layer underneath the epidermis. It is the 'storehouse' where all the things needed to keep skin healthy are kept: sweat glands that produce sweat (dissoved waste matter) to keep the body temperature steady; sebaceous glands which **lubricate** the skin with sebum and stop it from drying out and cracking – however, if the glands produce too much sebum, your skin becomes greasy; and also hair follicles with nerve endings.

Spots and acne

During adolescence – the early teenage years when the body undergoes a number of changes – the skin often becomes too oily. This can lead to blackheads, spots and acne. If you have acne, wash your face gently with a very mild soap and pat it dry with a towel. This will remove any grease without rubbing or irritating the skin.

If you have very bad acne, go to the doctor and ask him or her to prescribe a special cream or lotion.

Maintaining a healthy complexion

Rest, a healthy diet, exercise and knowing how to cleanse and generally take care of your skin will ensure a good clear complexion.

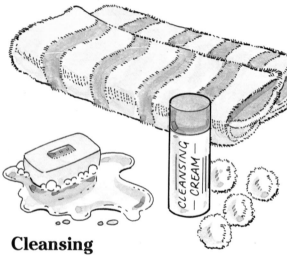

Cleansing

Soap and water is by far the most popular method used to cleanse the face, although it is not always suitable for every skin type. Some people prefer using one of the many cleansing creams widely available on the market.

Toners

The only disadvantage in applying a cream cleanser is that unless it is removed thoroughly a greasy film will remain over the face. That is why a cleansing process may be followed by the use of a toner to remove any dirt left over by the cleanser. Not only will it dissolve grease but it will also give skin an overall healthy feeling.

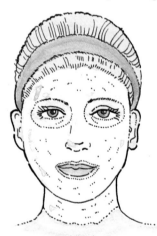

Moisturizers

These are very important to any make-up procedure. After cleansing and toning, moisturize the skin. Not only does it slow down the process of drying out but it ensures that it remains healthy and in top condition.

Face masks

Every few weeks or so a face mask can be very helpful. Not only will it remove make-up left on but it will also pep up the skin making it feel smooth.

Above Remove eye make-up carefully with an eye make-up remover pad.

Above If you prefer to cleanse with a cleansing cream or lotion, work in a generous amount with your fingertips.

Below Treat yourself to a face mask every few weeks to refresh your skin.

Above After refreshing your skin with a toner, apply some moisturizer.

Applying make-up

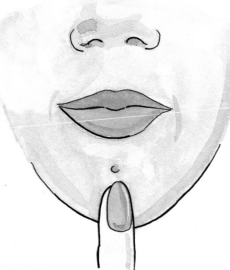

1 Concealer stick is a cover up cream which will hide spots. Choose a colour which is similar to the colour of your foundation and blend it in with your fingertips.

2 Foundation comes in stick or liquid form. It gives overall colour to your face, so the colour you choose should match your neck colour. Apply the foundation over your moisturizer. Blend it in carefully using your fingertips.

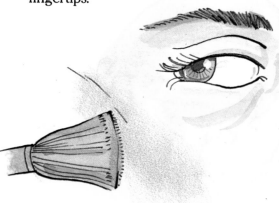

3 Powder gives foundation a perfect matte finish. Press it on with a puff and dust off any excess powder with cotton wool.

4 Blusher gives colour and shape to the face. Apply it to your cheeks with a brush. Use a deeper shade below your cheekbone to add shape to your face.

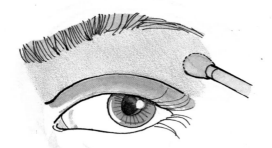

5 Eyeshadow comes in a wide variety of colours to suit every occasion. It comes in a cream or powder form. Choose natural colours for everyday wear, one darker than the other — coffee and beige, for example. Apply the paler shade over the entire eyelid, staring from the inner corner and working outwards. Apply a touch of the deeper coloured eyeshadow along the crease line.

6 Kohl crayons are available as soft pencils. They are used as colouring pencils to shape your eyes.

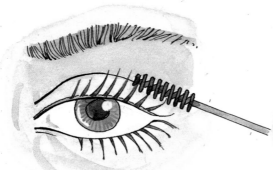

7 Mascara offers colour and thickness to your eyelashes. Apply an even coating of mascara to the upper lashes and then the lower ones. Leave to dry and then apply a second coat.

8 Lipstick gives colour and shine to your lips. Use a lip pencil to outline your lips and then fill them in with lipstick.

Wearing make-up to suit your face

To find out what kind of skin you have, look in a mirror and decide what is your skin colouring. For example:

● Do you have light coloured skin and hair? Do you find it hard to get a sun-tan and do you burn very easily in the sun? If so, you have FAIR skin.

● Do you have dark skin, eyes and hair? Do you tan easily without burning? If so, you have DARK skin.

● Are your hair, skin and eyes black or very dark? Do you not burn in the sun? If so, you have BLACK skin.

When you have decided which is your skin type, you can then choose make-up which is most suitable for you.

Below If you have light coloured eyes, skin and hair, you are fair skinned.

Dark skinned people have dark eyes and hair and tan easily.

If you have black or very dark eyes, skin and hair, and you do not burn in the sun, then your skin type is black.

Young people should aim to look as natural as possible, and should only wear make-up to **enhance** their features. It is a good idea to experiment with colours and ranges of make-up to find which suits you best. Always buy cheap make-up, because with many expensive products you are paying for the packaging. Take plenty of time to find out which colours of make-up suit your skin colouring and personality. Think about which are your good and bad features and discover how you can draw attention away from your bad points and make the best of your good ones.

Very few people are happy with the way they look. Most think that their nose is too big or their eyes are too small, or even that their mouth is too large.

Long nose– Reduce the size by applying a touch of highlighter to the tip of the nose and blending it in carefully.

Round face – Give the face more shape by shading the cheeks slightly. Apply blusher to a small section of the cheekbones, just under the corner of each eye.

Deep set eyes – Avoid wearing dark eye shadows. Soft shades such as apricot and cream are perfect.

Glasses – Choose strong, bold colours when selecting eye make-up.

Small mouth – Emphasize the corners of the mouth with lipstick.

Large mouth – Apply a small amount of foundation around the edges of the mouth. Blend it in until the actual line of the lips has disappeared, and then apply lipstick.

Party time

If you are going to a disco or party
then obviously your make-up is going
to be different from what you would
wear during the daytime.

1 After the usual cleansing routine
apply a layer of foundation and
powder — matching your skin colour
and tone — lightly over your face.
Brush on plenty of bright pink blusher
to highlight your cheekbones.

2 When deciding on the eyeshadow
consider your own eye colour, what
you are wearing and what would go
with it. Experiment with lots of colours
to get the right effect. Blue pearl
eyeshadow on the inner corner of your
eye and mauve under your brow bone
are a striking combination. To make
your eyes appear larger, apply a blue
kohl pencil line inside the bottom
eyelashes. Brush two coats of violet
mascara on to your eyelashes.

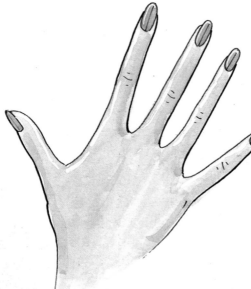

3 For two-tone nails, paint half of each
nail pink and allow to dry, then paint
the other half bright blue.

4 Outline the shape of your lips using
a blue lip pencil. Fill in the inside with
bright pink lipstick. As a final touch lip
gloss may be added to give an overall
shine.

Right Singer Whitney Houston wearing make-up at an awards ceremony.

Below Boy George (left) wearing bright, colourful make-up for a night out on the town with Freddy Mercury.

Everyday make-up

If you are going shopping or just going
to visit a friend it is best to wear light,
natural-looking make-up.

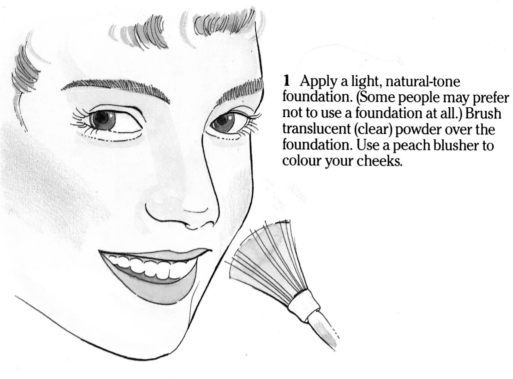

1 Apply a light, natural-tone
foundation. (Some people may prefer
not to use a foundation at all.) Brush
translucent (clear) powder over the
foundation. Use a peach blusher to
colour your cheeks.

2 Stroke pale blue eyeshadow on to
your eyelid and light pink shadow on
your brow. Use a pink kohl pencil to
draw a line above your top eyelashes.
Apply grey eyeshadow under your
lower lashes and then apply two coats
of black mascara.

3 Use a pale lipstick to colour
your lips.

Right Young women and girls do not need to wear much make-up, though blusher, lipstick and mascara can brighten up the face and outfit.

Everyday make-up should look fresh, natural and fun.

Glossary

Antiseptic A substance that destroys harmful germs.

Balanced diet Different kinds of food which together contain all the necessary vitamins, minerals and proteins to make us healthy.

Colourant Dyes used to change the colour of hair.

Conditioner A substance applied to hair to improve its overall look and condition.

Contagious A disease or illness that spreads quickly and easily from person to person.

Electrical appliances Tools which have a motor worked by electricity – for example, hair dryers or curling tongs.

Enhance To make something look better.

Follicles The little holes through which hair grows and which act as protectors.

Infections Diseases or illnesses that are easily passed on to other people.

Lubricate To spread oil or grease to make something smooth and supple.

Protein Any of a large number of substances which are vitally important to the growth and health of people and animals.

Sebaceous glands Small glands in the skin that release sebum (oil) into hair follicles and on to most of the body surface except for the soles of the feet and the palms of the hands.

Self-conscious Thinking too much about yourself and the impression you make on others.

Books to read

Be Beautiful. The Complete Guide to the Art of Make-Up (New Burlington Books, 1980)

Everygirl's Guide by Miriam Stoppard (Dorling Kindersley, 1987)

Girl, A Complete Guide to Looking Good and Feeling Good by Jan Shure (Piatkus, 1982)

Health and Exercise by Dorothy Baldwin (Wayland, 1987)

Health and Food by Dorothy Baldwin (Wayland, 1987)

Health and Hygiene by Dorothy Baldwin (Wayland, 1987)

Modelling and Beauty Care by Lucie Clayton (Made Simple Books, 1985)

The Hairstyle Haircare and Beauty Book by Linda Sonntag (The Apple Press, 1984)

You and Your Fitness and Health by Kate Fraser and Judy Tatchell (Usborne, 1986)

Index

Acknowledgements

The Publisher would like to thank the following for providing the pictures used in this book: Barnaby's Picture Library 6; Sally and Richard Greenhill 19; Penny Horton 5 (top); Duncan Raban COVER, 27 (bottom); Paul Seheult/Chapel Studios 8, 9, 10, 11, 12, 13, 14 15 (top), 17, 21, 24, 25, 29; Topham Picture Library 7, 27 (top); Wayland Picture Library 5 (bottom), 18 (top); Stephen Wheele 4, 16, 18 (bottom), 20, 22–3, 26, 28; ZEFA 15 (bottom). The Publisher would also like to thank Dominic Turner for styling the hair on pages 5 (top), 8, 9, 10 (bottom), 13, 17, 24.